Reaching for the Roses

Lead Me Safely Through the Perils in Life
Book 3

JANET F. ROBINSON

REACHING FOR THE ROSES
A book of poetry, scripture, and spiritual thoughts
Copyright © 2025 by Janet F. Robinson

All rights reserved. No part of this book may be reproduced in any form, whether by graphic, visual, electronic, film, microfilm, audio recording, or by any other means, without prior written permission of the author, except in the case of brief passages for critical reviews and articles.

Cover design: Sharon Kizziah-Holmes

Scripture quotations used in this book are from the King James Version of the Bible, The Book of Mormon Another Testament of Jesus Christ, and Doctrine and Covenants.

Scriptures from The Book of Mormon and Doctrine and Covenants
© By Intellectual Reserve, Inc. are used by permission.

Reaching for the Roses by Janet F. Robinson is neither made, provided, approved, nor endorsed by Intellectual Reserve, Inc. or The Church of Jesus Christ of Latter-day Saints. Any content or opinions expressed, implied, or included in or with the material are solely those of the owner and not those of Intellectual Reserve, Inc. or The Church of Jesus Christ of Latter-day Saints.

Printed in the United States of America

ISBN: 979-8-9861694-2-2

LIFE WITH ROSES

Scoffingly he asked, "Ye went out to seek,
so what did you find—
grasses greener,
a bed full of roses?"

Aye, sir, I have come back with my pockets empty.
I did not find fortune or fame,
but I have found something much better.
I found MYSELF!

Bah! YOU found yourself!
What kind of talk is that?
What is this world coming to?
Explain yourself!

I repeat,
"I have found myself.
I know who I am,
I know what I like and what I dislike.

I can make decisions.
I can think on my own.
I am free to be ME
and I, in turn, give you the freedom to be YOU.

I have no prejudices.
I believe in God.
I have love in my heart,
and I like myself.

Because I am at peace with myself
and I am my own person,
life is much sweeter
and more fulfilling.

The grass is greener,
the sky is bluer,
the hills are easier to climb,
and I can even see the roses."

Speak up! Roses, you say.
Have you no sense left?
I don't see any roses.
Bah! Humbug!

Oh! But they are there!
See! Over there! You must look for them.
To see the roses in life
is the ability to see good in a situation no matter how
bad it is.

It takes a Christian identity
to pick out the good in life.
This is what I have found,
and I will protect it from being taken away.

I will not let anyone
or anything
stand between me
and the roses in life.

To my husband, Gary:
You make me feel loved!

TABLE OF CONTENTS
Life With Roses
Preface
Introduction
Moving Forward 1
Freedom to Choose 11
Running the Race For Eternal Life 26
Embracing the Fullness of the Gospel 39
Keeping the Commandments of God 52
Living a Higher Law 61
Reaching for a Higher Plateau… 68
Closing Remarks 79
You've Been Good for Me 92
Acknowledgements 104
About the Author 105

Preface

THE THREE LOVES THAT HAVE IMPACTED MY LIFE

There are many loves in life, but these are the three loves that have had a major impact on me. If you have experienced all three of these loves, or if you have experienced only one of these loves, you have learned many life lessons.

I fell in love for the first time when I was in high school. We all remember our first love. I was shy, and I felt comfortable around my boyfriend. One of the many valuable lessons I learned from this love was to have more empathy and compassion for others.

My second love: When I was young, I fell in love with someone. He never kissed me, and he never ever held my hand. One day, I realized he did not feel the same about me, so I moved on. This experience taught me many priceless lessons about myself and life.

My third love: When Gary came into my life, I was not especially looking for love. He was a friend. We both had different religions, and we did not come from the same backgrounds, yet we could talk for hours. We discovered we had the same outlook on life, we had the same values, and we had a lot of things in common. We took each other by the hand, and we began to face the world together. I feel very fortunate I have found this third love in my life. This love has been a learning and a growing experience for me.

In this book, I share with you those things I have learned from this third love, share with you gospel truths that I have come to know in my heart are true and I have come to embrace with all my heart, share with you stories about my life, and share with you spiritual analogies I have made to my own life. These stories are not in chronological order.

Introduction

BE STILL AND LISTEN TO THE PROMPTINGS OF THE HOLY SPIRIT

During a difficult time, I felt the Spirit working in me. During this time, I found myself writing down thoughts that have helped me grow through the pain, thoughts whispered to me by the Spirit. He has been a comforter to me, He has been a teacher to me, and He has been my guide.

Later in life, I was introduced to the Fullness of the Gospel of Jesus Christ. I struggled with my strict protestant upbringing to know if I was being led in the right direction. After much prayer, seeking, and knocking, I found my answer in the thoughts I had previously written in *Undying Embers of God's Love* and *The Birth of a New Dawn in Me*. I know the same Spirit that taught me before was teaching me again. I realized that my deep faith and belief in Jesus Christ could never be taken away. My faith was a foundation for something higher in my spiritual life. I know the Spirit was prompting me and was leading me to a higher spiritual plateau of learning, growth, and understanding.

In this book, I refer to this higher plateau as reaching for the spiritual roses in my life.

~ ~ ~

By the power of the Holy Ghost ye may know the truth of all things.
Moroni 10:5

MOVING FORWARD

HOW TO DISCERN TRUTH?

We believe truth, or we believe a lie. God is the father of all truth. Satan is the father of all lies. God has sent us His Spirit to help us discern the difference between truth and lies. Truth gives us liberty or frees us. Lies keep us in shackles and enslave us.

It is impossible to progress (change to become a better person) unless we embrace the divine principle of forgiveness in our lives.

LETTING GO OF THE PAST

After having a heart-to-heart talk with my sister, Sharon, I have decided:
You are right, and I am wrong.

It is up to me to bury the past—all those times I felt unfairly treated by others. I should not keep bringing up those times over and over.

You have taught me that I should have resolved those conflicts at the time when they happened instead of years later. You have helped me understand that we should go directly to the person who has hurt us, resolve the conflict, forget it, and forgive.

This is a milestone in my life. I wish to consider yesterday gone, but today. . .
This day is a new beginning!

~ ~ ~

If ye forgive not men their trespasses,
neither will your Father forgive your trespasses.
Matthew 6:15

RECOGNIZING SOME STUMBLING BLOCKS TO PERSONAL AND SPIRITUAL GROWTH IN MY OWN LIFE

Today was the first day of my job at the bank, and I felt very insecure. I will always remember the kind words my supervisor, Shirley, said to me, "Whatever mistakes you make, just remember they have been made by someone before." That remark did not keep me from making a mistake, but it gave me the incentive to keep trying and to learn from my mistakes. Years later, I have always remembered Shirley's advice to me.

BEAUTY IN LIVING

My life became more beautiful
the day I began to face reality
that I am not perfect,
and I would never be perfect in this life.

I began to allow myself to make mistakes
so that I might grow as a person.
I still try my hardest, if not harder,
for now, I am taking on responsibilities.

It took this one step
in my life
to turn my thinking pattern around,
and life has become so beautiful!

On my desk, I have a quote rewritten in my own words:

"A friend is someone who accepts you as you are, he knows where you have been in life, he still likes you, and he gently encourages you to grow."

Today, a gentleman stooped over to read these words. He said, "The person who wrote this quote knew what he was talking about. I have had only one friend like that in my lifetime."

As I think about these thoughts, I feel my search has just begun to find that special person!

FACING OUR TRUE SELVES

I met someone today!
I will never feel it was by chance.
I believe it was God
who brought us together.

I see nothing fake or superficial
about this person.
He is a real person.
He is living reality.

We discussed the difference between
living reality and living fantasy.
We both agreed that living fantasy is much easier
than facing our true selves.

When we live fantasy, we try to fit ourselves into a mold
that we have created in our minds.
It is seeing only a part of ourselves—what we imagine
ourselves to be.
It is not facing the complete person.

When we live in reality,
we live the person God made us to be.
The person we show to the world
is the person we are.

We each have good and bad.
It is up to us as Christians to mature to a point so the good will gradually overcome the bad in our lives.

Realizing who the true person is inside of me has made all the difference in my own personal and spiritual growth.
Self-realization has helped me set personal goals to reach.
Self-realization has helped me see my weaknesses and the desire to rise to overcome them.

LETTING HIM LEAD

To my son and my daughter:

There have been many times I've unintentionally hurt you. I want you to know I am aware of your hurt.

There was the time your dad and I went through a divorce. Besides all the confusion you must have felt inside, I uprooted you. We moved in the middle of the school year. You had to say goodbye to your friends. You were faced with going to a new school and making new friends.

It has been five years now, and both of you have adjusted well. You have made friends, and both of you seem happy.

I announce tonight, "I have something important to talk to you about! Gary and I are planning to be married." With tears streaming down your face, you both ask, "Will we have to move?" There is a lump in my throat. I find it impossible to say anything. I know you already know the answer.

I do not know of any reason anyone should ask me what I see in you, but if they did, here is my ready reply:

I SEE IN YOU

A true, pure love for God,
a love that has grown through the years,
a love that is willing to answer His calling for you in life,
a love that has grown stronger through the storms and tears.

I see in you potential and maturity.
You have varied interests.
You have a knowledge of life that far surpasses anyone I have met,
and you feel good about yourself.

I see in you the ability to lead,
a willingness and a desire
to put the past behind
and move forward.

I see love for children,
a kindness toward mankind,
and a desire to LIVE Christ
every day of your life.

YOU ARE THE ONE!

You are many things to me.
I have complete confidence in you as a leader of our family.
I know I can turn to you any time, and you will be there for me.
I put my life and my future into your hands.

FREEDOM TO CHOOSE

PRIDE

God hates pride!
Pride blocks us from growing spiritually.
When we let go of pride, we become teachable.
Without pride in our life, we can grow spiritually beyond our traditional backgrounds.

~ ~ ~

*Are ye stripped of pride? I say unto you,
if ye are not ye are not prepared to meet God.*
Alma 5:28

One of the hardest things that I have ever done was to leave my traditional family church background. These are the Scriptures I read over and over during this emotional time:

> *There is a way which seemeth right unto a man, but the end thereof are the ways of death.*
> Proverbs 14:12

> *For my thoughts are not your thoughts, neither are your ways my ways, saith the LORD.*
> Isaiah 55:8

> *He that loveth father or mother more than me is not worthy of me: and he that loveth son or daughter more than me is not worthy of me. And he that taketh not his cross, and followeth after me, is not worthy of me. He that findeth his life shall lose it: and he that loseth his life for my sake shall find it.*
> Matthew 10:37-39

> *Wherefore, men are free according to the flesh; and all things are given them which are expedient unto man. And they are free to choose liberty and eternal life, through the great Mediator of all men, or to choose captivity and death, according to the captivity and power of the devil; for he seeketh that all men might be miserable like unto himself.*
> 2 Nephi 2:27

Everyone is given agency. We cannot grow spiritually unless we exercise agency to do good and seek righteous choices.

My definition of agency is:
Each of us is free to make good choices or bad choices. We are free to be a follower of Jesus Christ or not be a follower of Jesus Christ. Each of us is free to seek eternal life or not seek eternal life. We are given the freedom to make these choices for ourselves in life.

AGENCY

When my daughter was a senior in high school, she was selected to attend Girls State along with 600 girls across the state of Missouri.

For a whole week, these girls broke into groups and formed a mock government. They each belonged to a city. They elected a mayor, sheriff, House of Representatives, and governor.

My daughter asked me if I could pick her up on Friday night, which was Parent's Night. On Friday, I drove to be with my daughter at a college in central Missouri.

On Friday night the girls assembled in an auditorium. The governor of Missouri gave a speech, but the speech that influenced my thinking the most was given by Jenny, the outgoing girl's governor, as she gave a farewell message. She spoke of two principles relating to agency that have caused me to reflect on over the years. I would like to share these principles with you and apply them spiritually.

Jenny said her parents had given her roots and wings.

Roots

This is a list of my roots in the gospel my parents gave me when I was a child:

- Childhood memories
- Prayer
- Attending church meetings
- Visiting the sick
- Serving others

At this time in my life, I am striving to live the Fullness of the Gospel of Jesus Christ. I will add to this list:

- Tithing: We give at least 10% of our increased income.
- Family Home Evening: We set aside time on Monday nights (or another time) for family time together.
- Read scriptures daily
- Fasting: We have a Fast and Testimony Meeting on the first Sunday of each month. We fast (missing two meals) for twenty-four hours.
- Sustain church leaders
- Keep the Sabbath Day holy: We strive to worship by assembling ourselves on the

Sabbath Day and partake of the Sacrament.

Jenny made me realize one of the most important things I can give my children is roots in the gospel of Jesus Christ.

Wings

There comes a time, after we have given our children roots, we must stand back and give them wings.

Wings remind me of eagles. An eagle is one of the largest and most powerful birds in the world. Eagles soar gracefully in the air. Eagles have long been symbols of freedom and power.

We begin to exercise spiritual agency when we commit to living the principles of the gospel of Jesus Christ and striving to become Christlike.

Agency is a choice. If we choose the right direction, agency gives us freedom and power. If we make wrong choices and do not learn from our mistakes, we find ourselves going in the wrong direction. We stay in a state of sin, and we are like the baby bird who never learned to fly. We are in a fallen state, and we lose our freedom. We lose our power, and we become slaves to sin. We lose the privilege of spiritual agency until we seek repentance and, unless we are willing to change our heart, we cannot progress spiritually. We have the freedom to choose the right direction. We cannot grow spiritually unless we stay on the path of righteousness.

We are asked to prepare temporally and spiritually. We are given agency. The decision is ours to make—we can prepare, or we don't have to prepare.

PREPARING TEMPORALLY AND SPIRITUALLY

Then shall the kingdom of heaven be likened unto ten virgins, which took their lamps, and went forth to meet the bridegroom. And five of them were wise, and five were foolish. They that were foolish took their lamps, and took no oil with them: But the wise took oil in their vessels with their lamps. While the bridegroom tarried, they all slumbered and slept. And at midnight there was a cry made, Behold, the bridegroom cometh; go ye out to meet him. Then all those virgins arose, and trimmed their lamps. And the foolish said unto the wise, Give us of your oil; for our lamps are gone out. But the wise answered, saying, Not so; lest there be not enough for us and you: but go ye rather to them that sell, and buy for yourselves. And while they went to buy, the bridegroom came; and they that were ready went in with him to the marriage: and the door was shut. Afterward came also the other virgins, saying, Lord, Lord, open to us. But he answered and said, Verily I say unto you, I know you not. Watch therefore, for ye know neither the day nor the hour wherein the Son of man cometh.
Matthew 25:1-13

One time I attended a women's conference, and one of the speakers helped me understand this parable better. She said to be a nurse she had to prepare, go to school, work hard, and gain experience. She would not be able to hand over her knowledge and experience to someone who had no schooling to be a nurse or did not have the experience of being a nurse even if she wanted to.

At the beginning of the Covid era, I committed to prepare temporally.

From my research, these are questions that others have asked:
- What do we do if the electricity goes out?
- Where do we put our food storage when we don't have a lot of room?
- If we first pray for what to prepare for, as well as how to prepare, we will receive answers from Heavenly Father.

During this time, I listened to General Conference talks while I walked on my treadmill. General Conference is a worldwide gathering of members where church leaders share messages focused on the gospel of Jesus Christ.

I asked myself, "How can I prepare spiritually?" These answers came to me as I listened to these General Conference talks:

- If we want to progress, we must repent daily.
- We are to live our lives so we can feel the Holy Spirit.
- We are to strive to increase our faith in Jesus Christ.
- We are to increase our service to others.

~ ~ ~

For behold, this life is the time for men to prepare to meet God.
Alma 34:32

I can be a pioneer. I can blaze the way for others so they can follow Christ.

I will instruct thee and teach thee in the way which thou shalt go: I will guide thee with mine eye.
Psalm 32:8

MY THOUGHTS ON PIONEERING

I try to imagine what it was like to have been a pioneer trekking across to the west.

The early pioneers faced a long and dangerous journey by wagon trains across the Great Plains and the Rocky Mountains.

I learned from my research on pioneers that some pioneers loved adventure and some loved facing danger. Most pioneers faced danger and hardship because they were not content with what they had. They wanted a chance to improve their lives.

Pioneers usually traveled on trails that were blazed by explorers or fur traders.

The first pioneers hacked their way along steep, narrow trails. They had to know what to take with them and what to leave behind. Many set off on foot with little more than a rifle or an ax. Most had one or two pack animals and a wagon or cart. The long westward journey was generally made by several families traveling together. The pioneers helped one another on the trail and often shared supplies.

On the long journey west, the pioneers had one rule, and that rule was KEEP MOVING. They halted only long enough to repair equipment and buy supplies. They traveled fifteen to twenty miles a day.

I would like to apply these thoughts spiritually:

We are each traveling on a spiritual journey toward our return to Heavenly Father.

Christ has blazed a trail for us.

I am the way, the truth, and the life: no man cometh unto the Father, but by me.
John 14:6

At times, we find ourselves struggling to hack through crises in life. To grow spiritually, we must react in a Christlike manner when we find ourselves in different situations. This is a real challenge to ask ourselves, "How would Christ want me to act?" Most of us want to react to trials in the same manner as the world, and our heart becomes bitter.

On our spiritual journey, we must know what to take and what to leave behind. If we can learn to leave all the excess baggage we do not need, our journey will be easier and less burdensome. We must leave behind bad feelings toward others and let go of bad attitudes. We can do this by repenting every day of our life.

Our rule is to keep moving. Even when we are tired and discouraged, we keep moving so Satan does not overcome our lives.

Lastly, we are to band together and help each other along the way.

~ ~ ~

There is a scripture in Isaiah that is comforting to me. This scripture tells me if I stay close to my Savior and heed the promptings of the Spirit, He will help me through any danger and hardship I may face in this life. He will give me a chance to improve my life.

I will lead them in paths that they have not known: I will make darkness light before them, and crooked things straight. These things will I do unto them, and not forsake them.
Isaiah 42:16

Today, I can be a pioneer as I journey back to Heavenly Father. I can lead the way for others by following Christ.

If we let the Lord lead us back home to our Heavenly Father, He will lead us in paths where we have never been, He will light our way and give us understanding, our path will be straight, and He will always be with us.

These thoughts I have drawn from life on how we can be more effective in teaching others:

TEACHING OTHERS

We may have a calling as a teacher. We teach someone every day of our life. A child can teach us, a teacher teaches us, and our friends teach us.

My husband is a salesman. He is very good at what he does, and he enjoys his work. Over the years that I have known him, I have come to realize some of the things that have helped him be an effective salesman. He has developed a true love for his customers. He tells them true stories about his family and his friends. My husband tells them about his children and jokes he has played on our friends, Rich and Marianne. His customers relate to his true-life experiences. They tell him stories about their lives in return. He is honest in his business dealings with others. His customers have learned to trust him. They trust him to go to their supply room and make up their orders. He is dependable, reliable, and goes the extra mile for his customers. Before he leaves each morning, he gets on his knees and prays to Heavenly Father, and he invites the Spirit to be with him.

I will apply these same principles that have helped Gary be a good salesman to you and me as we teach others the gospel of Jesus Christ:

- Develop a true love for others.
- Read the scriptures—relate the stories in the scriptures to our own life.
- Be honest—be an example.
- Be dependable—go the extra mile.
- Pray and invite the Spirit into our lives.

~ ~ ~

And the Spirit shall be given unto you by the prayer of faith; and if ye receive not the Spirit ye shall not teach.
Doctrine and Covenants 42:14

A RIGHT DECISION?

After carrying through with my decision to resign from the job where I had been employed for several years, I suddenly realized I had accumulated a vast amount of knowledge that I would never be able to use again in my entire life.

This knowledge does not come into one's life overnight but through years of loyal dedication and many times going far beyond the call of duty.

I begin to feel a void in my life. I compare this feeling to a person who graduated from college and never used his college degree.

In reviewing my decision to resign and wondering if I acted too hastily, a phrase comes to my mind, and I stop to ponder, *"Is it really worth it?"*

I realized my decision was based on this one phrase: "The direction I found myself going, was it worth it?" This question can only be answered by one person and that person is myself—the frustrations, the long hours, and the feelings of hopelessness.

Maybe the answer would have been in the affirmative if there was some ray of hope ahead. I have worked through many challenges, and the only way I got through those challenges was hope—hope for a better life.

I find myself applying these thoughts spiritually. The direction we find ourselves going in this life—we should ask ourselves carefully, "Is it worth it? Is it for material wealth or gain? Is it for power and greed?

Or . . . were all those times we worked hard in our

church callings and rose to the occasion to serve others beyond the call of duty, all the times we made mistakes and learned by correcting our own mistakes, the vast amount of knowledge that we continually receive from Heavenly Father because He does give the gift of spiritual knowledge to His children when we ask Him. Were those times worth it?"

We know we have made the right choice because this path gives us hope. It is a ray that burns brightly—hope for eternal life.

After this life is over and when we find ourselves reviewing the choices we have made, will we be able to say? "It was worth it!"

RUNNING THE RACE
FOR ETERNAL LIFE

Wherefore, ye must press forward with a steadfastness in Christ, having a perfect brightness of hope, and a love of God and of all men. Wherefore, if ye shall press forward, feasting upon the word of Christ, and endure to the end, behold, thus saith the Father: Ye shall have eternal life.
2 Nephi 31:20

PRESSING FORWARD WITH FAITH IN JESUS CHRIST

During the last two weeks in February 1994, the eyes of the whole world were on Lillehammer, Norway, where the Winter Olympic Games were held. Gary and I watch the Winter Olympic Games as much as possible. All these competitors are reaching for the gold.

I find myself comparing living a worthy life to running a race in life and reaching for the prize of exaltation or eternal life.

> *Looking unto Jesus the author and finisher of our faith.*
> Hebrews 12:2

I asked Gary, "What does it mean when the scriptures say Jesus Christ is the author and finisher of our faith?" He said, "Jesus Christ was with us in the beginning, and if we finish the race, He will be with us at the end."

If we are willing to put into action the faith in this verse, the race for eternal life has begun. If we are to win a race, we must have a desire to win. Sometimes we settle for less. Sometimes we do not even try.

Who are the competitors in this race?

Will this race be easy?

I am reminded of the youth in our congregation, or ward, and how they have helped me. They teach me. We played ball during Super Saturday (a gathering of our youth from our Stake) one summer.

Our team lost. We had the choice of staying and playing again or giving up and going home. It was a warm day, and it would have been easier to go home. Cody, one of our youth, said, "I'm not a quitter!" That phrase has stayed with me at home and at my job.

My mom had a disease called Guillain-Barre Syndrome. She was paralyzed from her waist down. Through physical therapy, she regained the use of her body. She said to me, "My therapy is making me do something I cannot do."

In this race for eternal life, we must not quit. We must stretch to reach higher spiritually even if it seems impossible.

Who cheers us on? Is it our family, our friends, our brothers and sisters in Christ?

I must keep moving. There is no turning back. I must try my best to finish this race for eternal life.

Who will win this race? Those who endure to the end!

*Ye shall have hope through the atonement of
Christ and the power of his resurrection,
to be raised unto life eternal, and this
because of your faith in him.*
Moroni 7:41

THE POWER OF HOPE

My dad lives in his home. There are times he cannot dress himself, and he can barely walk with his walker. His decline came after he fell hitting his head. He fell when he was chasing a tire down the hill because he did not want the tire to hit his neighbor's house. As a result of his fall, Dad had a subdural hematoma on his brain which the doctors performed surgery to relieve the pressure. Afterward, he never fully regained complete balance even though he went through the physical therapy program at the nursing home.

I would like to share with you some of my visits to see my dad at the nursing home. As you enter, you see those that reach out to you and ask for you to help them. They want you to talk to them.

Looking around, you can see many have lost hope, whatever their hope might have been. I assume it could have been the hope of family and friends coming to see them, hope of becoming well, or hope of going home. Most residents do not have the hope of recovering, and most residents do not have the option of going home.

As I look around, I notice each person. There is

Edith. She is ninety-four years old. She has been a resident for ten years. My dad watched and learned from her how to make his wheelchair move faster. She moved her feet as if she were walking and moved the wheels of her chair with her hands.

On one visit to see Dad, we were in the lunch room. The sweetest lady and her husband were sitting with us at the same table. The wife lived in the assisted living part of the nursing home, and her husband lived in the nursing home next door. They would meet for lunch. Evidently, her husband had had a stroke. He would say the same thing over and over. Sometimes he would ask me, "Where do you live?" I would tell him. He would not say anything for about five minutes, and he would ask me again, "Where do you live?" He would also say to his sweet wife, "I want to go home. Please take me home." She would answer him, "This is our home now." She would continue, "When we both came here to live, I was determined I would be happy and make the best of it. We have good food, we have good care, and we have friends and family who come to visit us."

In thinking about my visits to see my dad, this thought came to me, "If someone were to tell the residents, you can be with your family and friends whenever you wish. You will soon be well, and you will be going home. I know you would see a light bulb come on inside of each person. They would be different people." I ask, "Why would they be different people?" The answer is that someone has given them hope.

The Atonement of Jesus Christ gives us hope for eternal life. The power of hope helps us through hard times. It is hope for each of us to have a better life after this life. We have hope that when we die, we will be with family and friends, we will not have any pain, we will no longer have diseases, and we will live with Heavenly Father.

I have learned:
- Hope is a gift.
- Hope fills us with happiness.
- Hope purifies us.

~ ~ ~

Every man that hath this hope in him purified himself.
1 John 3:3

Charity is the pure love of Christ. This love is self-giving, and it is the love Jesus Christ showed to others.

CHARITY

One year ago today, Gary and I gathered with my family in a hospital waiting room in Columbia, MO. We were there to support my sister, Brenda, as she gave a part of herself to her son. My sister gave her kidney to my nephew, Freddie, so he could have a better quality of life.

This is an example of a mother's love for her son, and it is also an example of my family's love for Brenda and Freddie by being with them during this time.

I think of Heavenly Father and the love He has for us. He expressed His love when He gave His only begotten son. He had no self-interest. Heavenly Father sacrificed by sending His son to earth so He might live, suffer, and die, and if we choose to believe in Christ, repent, and obey, we can have eternal life.

~ ~ ~

Charity is the pure love of Christ, and it endureth forever; and whoso is found possessed of it at the last day, it shall be well with him.
Moroni 7:47

Gary was gone all week, and these are some of the ways others have shown charity to me while he was gone:
- Someone helped me by shoveling snow off our driveway.
- A neighbor had someone remove the rest of the snow off our driveway.
- Someone fixed a meal and invited me over for dinner.
- Someone gave me a thank you note.
- My ministering sister (a sister who watches over me) visited me, and she brought me a surprise.
- Because we had lots of snow, someone took me to work and brought me home.

~ ~ ~

Pray unto the Father with all the energy of heart, that ye may be filled with this love.
Moroni 7:48

We are encouraged to read our scriptures daily.

READING OUR SCRIPTURES

Just recently I was checking my flowers in front of our house. I saw two fat yellow and green caterpillars eating on one of my plants. Without much thought, I picked both caterpillars, and I put them in my tub of soapy water I use when I pick Japanese beetles off my plants. These two caterpillars died immediately.

I asked myself, "What kind of caterpillars were they?" I researched and found they would have turned into beautiful black swallowtail butterflies. I felt bad because I had destroyed these caterpillars because of my lack of knowledge.

I will liken this story of the caterpillars and my lack of knowledge to all of us if we do not read our scriptures. If we put our scriptures on the shelf, we do not gain knowledge from the scriptures. Our scriptures are just sitting on the shelf not being used.

When I was a little girl, my mother read Bible stories to me and my siblings before bedtime. She read to us from a big thick book called Stories for Children from the Bible. Then, when I was older, I stayed overnight with my friend. She always read her scriptures before bedtime. Well, my friend was a big influence on me! I wanted to read my scriptures like her, so reading the scriptures became more important to me. When I was faced with making life-changing decisions, I searched my scriptures to find answers for me, and those answers helped me to know which direction I should take in life. When I married Gary, he was a big influence on me, and he encouraged me to read my scriptures daily.

Sometimes when I read my scriptures, I have a light bulb moment. I say, "I did not know that was in the scriptures!"

When this mortal life is over, when we meet Jesus face-to-face, we do not want to be without the knowledge we receive from our scriptures. We do not want to say, "I did not know, or no one told me."

I love my scriptures. In times of distress, they are a comfort to me. They are like a warm blanket wrapped around me. I have a desire to seek spiritual knowledge. I want to know Jesus Christ, and I want to hear His voice through the scriptures.

Enduring to the end reminds me of these thoughts I wrote after Gary and I visited with Jane several years ago.

ENDURING TO THE END

Jane was sitting at the kitchen table. One arm was resting on the table, and the other arm was lifted with her hand cupped to her forehead. We saw her as we drove into the driveway. She could have been praying. We hesitated before going inside to visit her. Her husband reassured us she would like visitors. After entering the room, it just took one glance at Jane to know death was near.

Gary and I were drawn to this woman today. We both had had a bad day.

Gary asked Jane, "By facing death, what are the things you have learned that would benefit the rest of us?" She replied, "To not be afraid of death." Jane felt the Lord was not ready for her to leave her home here on earth. When he was ready, he would call her home. She felt very strongly that her loved ones were waiting to receive her on the other side—her mother, father, and father-in-law. She gave us advice to study the scriptures.

I have known Jane for two years. When I first met her, I sensed God had blessed her with the gift of knowledge. After I knew Jane better, I realized this knowledge went beyond the scriptures. She also had knowledge about life itself.

Jane is a perfect example of a woman who has

lived graciously, and now she is dying graciously. Through all her pain, I have not heard her complain once. She accepts the pain and is waiting to be called home.

Gary and I both left that evening with a happy heart. She had cheered us both—this brave, dying woman.

On the way to Springfield one day, we passed a sign that read "To have the rainbow, we must first have the rain." Gary turned to me and said, "That is true, isn't it?"

Through all the storms I have been through, I have had the hope of a rainbow. This hope has helped me get through some difficult circumstances. I like to think my rainbow is eternal life.

Embracing the Fullness of the Gospel of Jesus Christ

Four Principles of the Fullness of the Gospel of Jesus Christ

Faith in Jesus Christ
Repent of all our sins
Baptism by immersion
Receive the gift of the Holy Ghost

FAITH IN JESUS CHRIST

When I first met Gary, he was an art student. Before we were married, he painted a picture. I like this picture for two reasons: I like what I see, and this painting was a gift to me.

I will describe this painting to you. It is rather large—3 feet x 2 ½ feet. It is very simple—there are two eagles flying over a mountain.

Through the years, this painting has come to have special meaning in my life. I would like to share some thoughts and feelings I have had as I look at this painting.

Sometimes as I stand looking at this painting, I am reminded of this scripture:

They that wait upon the LORD shall renew their strength;
they shall mount up with wings as eagles;
they shall run, and not be weary;
and they shall walk, and not faint.
Isaiah 40:31

As I study and try to know the meaning of this verse, a thought comes to me that this Scripture means: When we try to do the will of the Lord, we develop our faith and trust in Him. When our faith is rooted and grounded in Jesus Christ our Savior, He has promised us we will be able to mount up with eagle wings and fly spiritually on a higher plateau.

I ask myself, "How do I reach this higher spiritual plateau?" I think of this scripture found in Matthew 7:7 *Ask, and it shall be given; seek, and ye shall find; knock, and it shall be opened unto you.*

There are times I look at this painting, and I don't feel much like flying today. These are the times when I feel the whole bottom has dropped out of my life. For each of us, the struggle may be something different. Maybe we are having a financial crisis, maybe our marriage is falling apart, or maybe it is the death of a loved one. We are experiencing the lowest of lows, and we feel we cannot go on. We find ourselves struggling to cope with life.

I have recently accepted the Fullness of the Gospel of Jesus Christ in my life. Gary and I are striving to make changes. We find ourselves learning, studying, and growing spiritually. We listen to each other, and we communicate with each other our spiritual thoughts. We are helping each other.

Now, as I look at this painting, I see something I have never seen before. This time I see two people climbing upward hand in hand. I know the journey that lies before us will be long and difficult. I have the hope of reaching a higher spiritual plateau.

The Spirit of the LORD....has wrought a mighty change in us, or in our hearts, that we have no more disposition to do evil, but to do good continually.
Mosiah 5:2

~ ~ ~

I know I will be able to fly spiritually! I will be able to mount up with wings as eagles, and when the storms of life come down on me, I shall run and not be weary, and I shall walk and not faint.

The Atonement of Jesus Christ not only gives us forgiveness for our sins, but the Atonement of Jesus Christ can help us overcome, help us change, and we can be strengthened.

THE ATONEMENT OF JESUS CHRIST

Gary and I served in the Fort Leonard Wood Base congregation for eighteen months. When I first attended Relief Society, the Relief Society President told me sometimes we would have one person or no one or sometimes we would have a whole platoon of soldiers attend. Relief Society is an organization for women. Its purpose is to provide service, create sisterhood, teach, and share the gospel of Jesus Christ.

~ ~ ~

The following stories are examples of how the Atonement of Jesus Christ helps us change, overcome, and be a stronger person:

The Atonement of Jesus Christ Can Help Us Change to Be a Better Person

One Sunday, a member of the General Authority Seventies (a church leader who teaches the gospel of Jesus Christ throughout the world) visited Fort Leonard Wood. He drew a vertical line on the blackboard. This line represented the iron rod or the word of God. When he was young, he did not have the gospel of Jesus Christ in his life, and he was living far from the iron rod. He was introduced to the gospel of Jesus Christ and was baptized. He then lived closer to the iron rod, but he still did some of the things he wanted to do but shouldn't. Now, later in life, he has fully embraced the gospel of Jesus Christ, and he is trying to keep all of God's commandments. He is now living in line with the iron rod. He is teaching his children the blessings that come from living all the gospel of Jesus Christ.

The Atonement of Jesus Christ Can Help Us Overcome Bad Things That Happen to Us

On Sundays, the soldiers took turns giving talks during Sacrament. One of the soldiers gave the following talk: When he was a boy, his mom was addicted to drugs, and she was gone for days. His baby brother was left in his care, and sometimes they were hungry because there was no food in their house. Later in life, he was introduced to the gospel. He went on a church mission, and he was sealed to his wife in the temple (to be sealed in the temple ensures that death cannot separate loved ones if the person is sealed in the right place and by the right authority).

This story is an example of how a soldier overcame some very difficult circumstances in his childhood.

The Atonement of Jesus Christ Helps Us to Be Strong

The burdens which were laid upon Alma and his brethren were made light; yea, the Lord did strengthen them that they could bear up their burdens with ease, and they did submit cheerfully and with patience to all the will of the Lord.
Mosiah 24:15

The Lord could have removed the burdens of Alma and his people; instead, He strengthened them to bear their burdens with ease. They did not complain, but they submitted cheerfully and patiently to the will of the Lord. The Atonement of Jesus Christ also gives us strength to endure pains and afflictions and temptations of every kind because our Savior also took upon Him the pains and the sicknesses of His people.

~ ~ ~

…. he will take upon him the pains and the sicknesses of his people.
Alma 7:11

> *If men come unto me, I will show unto them their weakness. I give unto men weakness that they may be humble; and my grace is sufficient for all men that humble themselves before me; for if they humble themselves before me, and have faith in me, then will I make weak things become strong unto them.*
>
> Ether 12:27

For several years, Gary and I conducted an addiction recovery meeting. The above scripture was in our manual, and when we came to this scripture, everyone took turns sharing their thoughts on what this scripture meant to them.

This is my understanding of this scripture:

Each of us has been given a weakness or weaknesses. Our weaknesses can become a good thing for us. First, we must realize what our weaknesses are. To know, we must come unto Christ and ask what our weaknesses are. Through His Spirit, He will show us our weaknesses. When we know what our weaknesses are, our weaknesses humble us. We know we need to work to overcome them.

We ask Heavenly Father to help us overcome our weaknesses. We realize it is only through the Atoning Blood of our Savior Jesus Christ that we can change. We put our faith and trust in Him. This change may take a long time or even a lifetime.

We know we have changed when we recognize our weaknesses have become a strength to us.

There was a time in my life, I fell off the wagon of trying to live for Christ and be an example for Him. I became angry with God because my life was not going in the direction I wanted. Because I was angry with God, I started taking the easier road and not the harder, higher road. I found myself following the crowd, and I began doing those things that were out of character for me. I found myself moving further and further away from truth. I knew in my heart I had to get right with God, and I had to get back on the path to eternal life. This was the only way I would ever feel peace again.

~ ~ ~

Joy shall be in heaven over one sinner that repenteth.
Luke 15:7

REPENTANCE

While Gary and I were building our house, we lived in our friend John's little house in the country. This two-story house has white siding, the main floor is one room, and it has an upstairs and a basement. On the front of this house, there is a porch with a red bench. I was told this little house used to be an apple mill.

Before we moved in, John recognized the need to clean the house. He worked hard taking out stuff he had stored in it. I am assuming some of it was junk since he made several trips to his junkyard. John made repairs to this house.

When you enter this little house, you will notice the wood ceilings and the open beams. John's wife and his daughter worked hard stripping the ceilings and refinishing them. The ceilings are beautiful.

Three things from this story remind me of repentance:
- Recognizing the need to clean up our lives.
- Making repairs or mending the wrongs we have done.
- Looking for the beauty that comes from repentance.

We must recognize the need to repent. We must feel sorrow for our sins. We must feel sincere sorrow for what we have done. We must feel our sins are terrible. We must forsake our sins. Whatever we have done to sin, we must stop and not do it again. We must confess our sins. We must make restitution. As much as possible, we must make right any wrong we have done.

We must forgive others. A vital part of repentance is forgiving those who have sinned against us. I believe the Lord will not forgive us unless our hearts are fully cleansed of all hate, bitterness, and bad feelings toward others.

This promise is given to us:

> *Though your sins be as scarlet, they shall be as white as snow.*
> Isaiah 1:18

Baptism is the gate we enter to the covenant path to eternal life.

BAPTISM AND RECEIVING THE GIFT OF THE HOLY GHOST

I would like to tell you a story I read recently from my scriptures, and I would like to share with you the things I learned from this story.

Abinadi was a prophet of God. He prophesied to the people. He told them to repent and turn to the Lord their God, and if they did not repent, they would be brought into bondage, and they would be afflicted by their enemies.

Alma was a priest to the wicked King Noah, and he had not been taught to live righteously. But Alma believed the words Abinadi taught the people. Alma believed in Jesus Christ. Alma repented of his sins and iniquities and went about privately teaching the words of Abinadi. Many of the people believed in his words. They went to a place called Mormon. Alma preached unto them repentance and redemption and faith in the Lord. Alma was baptized in the waters of Mormon.

Alma said unto the people, *Behold, here are the waters of Mormon… and now, as ye are desirous to come into the fold of God, and to be called his people, and are willing to bear one another's burdens, that they may be light; Yea, and are willing to mourn with those that mourn; yea, and comfort those that stand in need of comfort, and to stand as witnesses of God at all times and in all things, and in all places that ye may be in, even until death, that ye*

may be redeemed of God, and be numbered with those of the first resurrection, that ye may have eternal life. Now I say unto you, if this be the desire of your hearts, what have you against being baptized in the name of the Lord, as a witness before him that ye have entered into a covenant with him, that ye will serve him and keep his commandments, that he may pour out his Spirit more abundantly upon you?
Mosiah 18:8-10

~ ~ ~

This story about Alma contains four principles of the Gospel that are essential for us to return to Heavenly Father:
- Alma listened, he believed, and he had *faith* in Jesus Christ.
- Alma *repented* of his sins and iniquities.
- Alma was *baptized* in the water.
- Alma *received the gift of the Holy Ghost*.

I can feel the power of the Atonement of Jesus Christ as I read this story. Alma had a mighty change of heart, and he changed from within. He wanted to do what was right.

This story contains our baptismal covenants for us today:
- Be willing to bear one another's burdens.
- Yea, and are willing to mourn with those who mourn.
- Yea, comfort those who stand in need of comfort.
- Always stand as witnesses of God, and in all things, and in all places.

Keeping the Commandments of God

And moreover, I would desire that ye should consider on the blessed and happy state of those that keep the commandments of God. For behold, they are blessed in all things, both temporal and spiritual; and if they hold out faithful to the end they are received into heaven, that thereby they may dwell with God in a state of never-ending happiness.
Mosiah 2:41

Thou shalt love the Lord thy God with all thy heart, and with all thy soul, and with all thy mind, and with all thy strength: this is the first commandment. The second is . . . Thou shalt love thy neighbor as thyself.
Mark 12:30-31

THE PURE LOVE OF CHRIST

In our home, we have a picture that serves as a reminder of our Savior's love for my family and me. As I look at this picture, I see a house with flowers and hearts. It reads, "Most of all, let love guide your life."

The Importance of the Pure Love of Jesus Christ in Our Lives

Love is a commandment of Heavenly Father.
Love is a path to peace (no contention).
Without it we are nothing.

This love is a gift from Heavenly Father.
 One has not truly loved
until this selfless love is experienced.

~ ~ ~

Charity is the pure love of Christ, and it endureth forever; and whoso is found possessed of it at the last day, it shall be well with him.
Moroni 7:47

Thou knowest the commandments, Do not commit adultery, Do not kill, Do not steal, Do not bear false witness, Honour thy father and thy mother.
Luke 18:20

HONOR THY MOTHER

I remember Mother's Day when my son was in the sixth grade. He gave me a huge Mother's Day card. He said, "Mom, I didn't even read this card—I just picked out the biggest card I could find."

I also have memories of my mother, who has passed away. One time I thought of five words that describe her.
- Work
- Quilting
- Happy
- Spiritual
- Gardener—My mother was an avid gardener. She planted seeds. She cultivated, nourished, and watered the seeds, and then she watched her garden grow. She always seemed to have a bountiful harvest which she shared with others.

Spring is the time to beautify our homes. This is the time of year we plant seeds, we plant our gardens, and we plant flowers and shrubs.

At some point in life, the gospel is planted in our heart as a seed is planted in the earth. If the seed is nourished with lots of love, tender care, understanding, gentleness, and watered with kindness, the seed of the gospel will grow.

> *Behold, there went out a sower to sow... some fell by the way side, and the fowls of the air came and devoured it up. And some fell on stony ground where it had not much earth.... when the sun was up, it was scorched... because it had no root... some fell among thorns and the thorns... choked it... other fell on good ground and did yield fruit.*
> Mark 4:3

Jesus taught in parables. Jesus told stories and related the stories to spiritual truth so His listeners could easily understand what He was saying.

I have another memory of my son in the 1st grade. He was so excited to plant a sprout he had found in the ditch. I never thought much about this small sprout until a tree began to grow. We moved a few years later, and at this time, the tree had grown into a small tree. Several years later, Gary took me to that same house I had lived in long ago, and there was a huge tree in the backyard. I was amazed the small sprout had grown into a huge tree.

My mother planted seeds not just because she loved gardening, but she worked hard so we would have food for the winter. She had a purpose.

We also have a purpose for sowing seeds of the gospel of Jesus Christ (good seeds):

He which soweth sparingly shall reap also sparingly; and he which soweth bountifully shall reap also bountifully.
2 Corinthians 9:6

HONORING MOTHERS

How do we show honor? In answering this question, five suggestions come to my mind on how I honor my mother.

Time
Talk often to Mother and listen to her.

Express Love and Devotion to Your Mother
I have a memory of my son when he was in the fourth grade. I had just finished reading him a book. Afterward, he looked up at me with the sweetest and most admiring look and said, "Mom, you are the best mom in the whole world." I will always remember him expressing his love for me as long as I live.

Service
We honor our mother by giving service to her.

Money
Give a gift! I only want a small token of appreciation, maybe a card or artwork. It does not have to cost very much. Our daughter, Andrea, is very creative. She always has something to give me on Mother's Day. If she does not have any money, she makes me a gift.

Presence

Every mother wants to be with her children. We honor our mother when we show up for a special occasion.

~ ~ ~

How can we honor our Savior? We can apply these same five suggestions when we honor our Savior.

Time

We honor our Savior when we take time to read our scriptures, take time to pray and talk to our Heavenly Father, and when we are quiet and listen to the Spirit.

Love and Devotion

We honor our Savior when we express our love for Him—we may bear our testimony of Jesus Christ to someone. We may look up at the sky and say, "I do love you, Heavenly Father, and thank you for sending your Son to earth so that I have this hope of eternal life."

Service

When we give service to others, we are also giving service to God.

Money

We honor our Savior when we pay our tithes or use our money to help someone in need.

Presence

Just as a child honors his mother when he is present, we honor our Savior when we are present to assemble on the Sabbath Day.

~ ~ ~

If you want to make your mother happy today, remember to take time for her out of your busy schedule, express your love and devotion to her, spend a little of your hard-earned money on a tiny gift, and be with her today. She will reward you, I guarantee, with love and joy.

If we take time for our Savior on the Sabbath day to express our love and devotion, give back to Him some of our hard-earned money, and be present, I know He will bless us beyond all our highest expectations. He will bless us in ways we have never dreamed.

LIVING A HIGHER LAW

It is our choice—we have agency. We can live a higher law, or we can live a lower law. If we choose to live a higher law, we will be blessed with spiritual learning, growth, and understanding.

~ ~ ~

The Law of Chastity, The Law of the Fast,
The Law of Tithing, Keep the Sabbath Day Holy,
Word of Wisdom, Serving Others

THE LAW OF CHASTITY

We live the Law of Chastity so we can be clean and pure from sin. Those who break the Law of Chastity can be forgiven by Heavenly Father if they repent.

THE LAW OF THE FAST

Each month we observe a fast day. We do not eat or drink anything for two consecutive meals. We fast with a purpose, and we begin and end our fasting with a prayer.

We fast when we seek answers from Heavenly Father when we need help or we need to know which direction we should take in life. Fasting helps us draw closer to Heavenly Father.

The word tithe means one-tenth.

THE LAW OF TITHING

We tithe one-tenth of our increased income. When we pay our tithes, we have been promised to be blessed both materially and spiritually.

~ ~ ~

> *Let him give; not grudgingly, or of necessity:*
> *for God loveth a cheerful giver.*
> 2 Corinthians 9:7

KEEP THE SABBATH DAY HOLY

The Sabbath Day is a day of rest, a day to partake of the Sacrament, a day to serve others, and a day to have family strengthening activities.

We strive to observe this commandment from Heavenly Father.

~ ~ ~

Remember the sabbath day, to keep it holy.
Exodus 20:8

WORD OF WISDOM

The Word of Wisdom is a law of health. We strive to eat only food that is good for us and not take anything into our body that is harmful to us. Those who obey the Word of Wisdom are promised increased health, wisdom, knowledge, and protection.

SERVING OTHERS

Neal visited our ward today. He is a counselor to our stake president. A stake president is over several wards or congregations. I jotted these words down from Neal's talk that he gave in Sacrament meeting:

"When we serve others, we serve them because we are trying to be like Jesus. We are not trying to earn our way to heaven, but we serve others as He served others. When we serve others, we find ourselves increasing our ability to love."

There are two people in my life that have been a prime example to me as they serve others:

- My sister, Brenda, is the most unselfish person I have ever met. I truly believe she has committed her life to helping others.
- Marie is another person that has been an example to me as she unselfishly gives to others. When she sees a need, she is always there. There are many times I have seen her just show up to lend a helping hand without being asked.

Reaching for a Higher Plateau of Learning, Growth, and Understanding

Covenants, Temple, Priesthood, The Great Plan of Happiness

~ ~ ~

Happy is the man that findeth wisdom, and the man that getteth understanding.
Proverbs 3:13

I consider my life a journey that always leads me upward to my heavenly home. I wish to share the lessons I have learned along the way. I learn best from my own experiences in life.

WHAT IS A COVENANT?

What is a covenant, and why do we make covenants? What are the blessings we receive from keeping our covenants?

Most of the time, you must tie me to a chair to get me to sit down. Suddenly, I had to lie with my head facing down for two weeks. I wondered about a prayer Gary gave. He asked the Lord to help me enjoy this time. I thought, "What! Enjoy this?" Then I thought, "OK, I will try to enjoy this quiet time I have been given."

Just recently, I went to my eye doctor because I was having trouble seeing in my right eye. After running an OCT scan, my doctor seemed rather excited and told me I had a hole in the macula of my eye. Fast forward—he sent me to a surgeon and two days later I had a surgery called a vitrectomy. My surgeon explained to me she had inserted a gas bubble in my eye. I had to lie in a face-down position for two weeks so the bubble would be over part of my eye to help in healing.

As I shared my news with my family and friends, my sister-in-law said she thought it would be hard to keep my head down for two weeks. I told my sister-in-law, "I have been asked to keep my head down for the healing of my eye, and I will do it."

My thoughts turned to this story from the Old Testament:

> *Naaman, captain of the host of the King of Syria, was a great man with his master, and honourable, because by him the LORD had given deliverance unto Syria; he was also a mighty man in valour, but he was a leper.*
>
> 2 Kings 5:1

Elisha (a prophet) told Naaman he could be healed, but he had to go dip in the River Jordan seven times. The River Jordan had dirty water, and Naaman let pride get in his way. He did not want to get in the dirty water even though it was a simple task. He later decided to do what he was asked, and he was healed.

I relate this story to you because it is an unspoken covenant I made with my doctor. He told me the plan, what I had to do, and if I did it, I could be healed.

In thinking about the covenant I made with my doctor, I am feeling the blessing of doing what my doctor asked me to do. I am beginning to have sight in my eye. I feel grateful.

These are three important covenants we make:
- Baptism
- Sacrament
- Temple Covenants

Before I accepted the Fullness of the Gospel of Jesus Christ, I was happy. I saw no reason to change. I was a protestant. I had a testimony of Jesus Christ. I did not want to separate myself from my parents and my siblings. I was happy living my life as it was.

What was it that made me want to change?

The missionaries triggered in me this feeling: I reached a point in my life that I wanted to live a higher law, a higher standard of living, and a higher level of learning—a higher law that I make covenants with my Lord so that I can receive the promised blessings He has promised me.

Heavenly Father has told us the plan, what we must do, and if we do it, we will be blessed.

HOW HAS ATTENDING THE TEMPLE STRENGTHENED MY MARRIAGE?

When Gary and I were married, we were married in a civil ceremony. Before we were married, I remember talking to John. He showed me a picture of a temple, and he shared with me that couples go to the temple to be married so they can be sealed for time and eternity by someone who has the authority to do so. He said being married in a civil ceremony meant I would only be married to Gary until we die in this mortal life—until death do we part.

As I look back over the years, I ask myself, "How has attending the temple blessed my life and strengthened my marriage?" Four words come to my mind, "unity, trust, hope, and protection."

Unity

When I married Gary, we had many things in common. We thought so much alike. But there was one thing missing for both of us. It was unity in our belief. I was a protestant, and I could not see the whole picture as he saw it. I did not know that. I did have a strong testimony of my Lord and Savior Jesus Christ.

We did not have spiritual unity in our home. It was when I let go of pride, I allowed myself to become teachable. I was baptized, and a year later, we were sealed for all time and eternity in the Dallas temple.

Trust

My favorite Scripture is:

Trust in the LORD with all thine heart; and lean not unto thine own understanding. In all thy ways acknowledge him, and he shall direct thy paths.
Proverbs 3:5-6

I have read this Scripture many times, especially those times I was not sure which direction I should take.

By attending the temple with my husband and making and keeping sacred covenants, I have learned to trust. Trust in myself, trust in my husband, and trust in the Lord.

- Trust in myself that I can become a better person.
- Trust in my husband—his integrity, his intelligence, his abilities, his potential.
- Trust in the Lord that He will direct my path.

Hope

I hope to be able to live in the presence of Heavenly Father after this life.

Protection

Several years ago, Gary and I traveled to visit our daughter Andrea. Andrea is in the Air Force and, at the time, she was living in England.

Gary and I are not world travelers. We were left to ourselves to find our way around as our daughter could not take off work. We could not drive as the English drive on the opposite side of the road. We found it very hard to communicate because we did not understand what the English were saying. The English talk very fast, and they have a heavy accent. Early in the week, Gary and I walked to a grocery store only a few blocks away. We purchased some items, and when we went to pay for them, the clerk asked us a question. We could not understand her. She asked us the question three times, and we just stood and looked at her. Suddenly it dawned on us she was saying, "Do you want a bag?" We were so flustered we started to go out the wrong door, and an alarm went off. We found ourselves feeling uneasy and not sure of ourselves.

We found the bus stop. The next day we took the bus to London to visit some tourist sites. This was shortly after 911, and there were terrorist attacks in England at this time. When Gary and I were there, we did not feel comfortable. Toward the end of the week, we decided to take the bus to the London temple. Once there, I felt the overwhelming feeling of being safe from the evil influences from the outside world.

Now when I attend the temple, I still feel safe. I carry that feeling with me when I go home, and I feel safe in my marriage. I feel safe from the evil influences from the outside world.

All these feelings of unity, trust, hope, and protection are some of the ways that have strengthened me and my marriage when I attend the temple.

BLESSINGS OF A TEMPLE MARRIAGE

Gary and I were sealed in the Dallas Temple.
I remember holding Gary's hand while we were kneeling at the altar.

A temple worker sealed us together for all time and eternity. This ceremony must be performed by someone who has sealing power. He holds the priesthood—the priesthood is the power and authority of God to perform this sacred ordinance. The temple is the only place where this holy ordinance can be performed.

I remember making marriage covenants before God. We were promised blessings depending on our obedience to the laws of God.

I would like to bear my testimony that our marriage has been blessed. We have been blessed in this earthly life, we know we will be blessed in the life hereafter, and we know we can be a family forever.

These thoughts are taken from my journal: "It was a good feeling to be sealed for all time and eternity to the man I love and the person I want to be with forever. Our relationship is a growing relationship. We help each other. He counsels me and I counsel him. We have helped each other grow as people and grow spiritually."

A HIGHER LEVEL OF LEARNING

I was listening to the radio recently, and a commercial came on about a home improvement store that was advertising new wood cabinets. In trying to sell their product, this was the phrase they used "Put happy back into your life"!

On the way to the Kansas City temple, we passed by another sign. The picture on this sign is a kitchen remodel. The sign reads "Happy wife—Happy life"! I have come to realize that keeping the commandments of God lead me to a happy life, and it is not wood cabinets, not a new kitchen, and not a new car or a new truck.

As I get closer, I can see the temple from a distance. It is beautiful, and it stands tall and majestic. As I go inside, I feel safe and sheltered from the storms that I have. I feel this is the place I can come to receive any answers I need from Heavenly Father, especially those things that weigh heavily on me from within. I feel the Spirit. I feel peace.

As I go through the temple session, I receive instructions for the Plan of Salvation or the Great Plan of Happiness.

The Plan of Salvation helps me answer these questions:

Where did I come from?
Why am I here on earth?
Where am I going after this life?

THE PLAN OF SALVATION OR THE GREAT PLAN OF HAPPINESS

Talk by Gary Robinson at our friend Larry's Funeral

We are here to honor my friend, Larry. I hope to have the Spirit with me so I can honor him properly.
Where did we come from?
Let me tell you about his life. Larry came from the presence of his Father in Heaven. We all did—Larry, you, and I. Larry was made in His image. We all were. Larry was made to be like our Father—to become like Him.
In Heaven, we all possessed different talents and abilities for different callings on earth. Larry was taught in heaven as far as he could progress. We all had to leave to be able to continue growing and to be tested.
Why are we here?
Our Father in Heaven called a Grand Council to present His plan:
- Come to earth
- Choose good or evil
- Risk becoming lost
- Learn faith
- Learn to use our agency
- Learn to use challenges to improve us and not defeat us.

We all shouted with joy when we chose to come to earth. We knew we would risk everything if we didn't do it right.

Larry's life was, at times, very hard. He struggled with alcohol. His grandma taught him to love the Bible and to be deeply concerned about spiritual things.

AA, among other things, helped Larry with his problem with alcohol.

The turning point in Larry's life was when he received a priesthood blessing from Arlen and me with Arlen being the voice. Larry felt the Spirit very strongly when he received this blessing. Shortly after, he was baptized and joined the church, and he became born again. He served willingly because he loved Jesus. He was not working his way to heaven, but he truly loved others. He wanted to live as Jesus would have him live.

Larry repented very sincerely and took it seriously. If Larry had a fault, he found it hard to forgive himself for his past.

Larry served well, even when he didn't feel well.

Larry passed away this Easter weekend. His mortal struggle is over. It was an honor for him to die on this weekend.

Where are we going?

Where is Larry now?

He is in the Spirit world waiting, working, learning, and resting from all cares and sorrow. His body isn't hurting anymore. He isn't far from us. He has the same attributes and attitudes he had here which are love for others and devotion. I believe he is in paradise doing the Lord's work. He is a priesthood holder and will continue to do priesthood work.

Closing Remarks

In our congregations, we do not have a paid ministry. The members are asked to give talks (like sermons) in our Sacrament meetings.

This Sacrament talk was given by Janet Robinson:

SUSTAINING MY HUSBAND

There are many ways we can sustain our husband. I have chosen five ways that I sustain Gary:
- I understand my calling from Heavenly Father to be a help meet to Gary. I am sustaining my husband when I am a helper to him A help meet is a companion that is suitable for his/her spouse. A help meet protects, helps, and does what the other cannot do.

And the LORD God said, It is not good that the man should be alone; I will make him an help meet for him.
Genesis 2:18

- All of us have many reasons in our lives why we could become bitter people. Many years ago, I took this challenge. I said, "Janet, you can become a better person, or you can become a bitter person." It would be left up to me. It would be my decision to make! I have a desire to become better and work to become my best. I have learned our husbands will love us more if we strive to be better. Our husbands will love us less if we become bitter.

Gary and I sit with Jim at the Senior

Center. Have you ever noticed his positive outlook on life and his fun and caring nature? I asked Jim this question, "Why do you think the Atonement of Jesus Christ instills in us a desire to become better?" I like his answer, "The Atonement of Jesus Christ liberates us and sets us free from sin and guilt. We can be happy and free, which gives us a desire to study, learn, and grow, and in turn, helps us to become better people. As a result of striving to become better, I want to use my priesthood more in my life."

- I am a companion and a friend to my husband. Currently, he is living with physical limitations. We are friends, we have long talks, and we still have fun together!
- I strive to keep my house clean and in order. We have taken steps to watch TV less. We have committed to studying the new church home study, Come Follow Me, together. We both strive to keep negative influences out of our home. It is important for both of us to feel the Spirit in our home. I sustain him in this.

- I love and respect Gary for who he is. I realize neither of us is perfect, nor will we ever be perfect in this life, but I respect him especially because he is trying his best through difficult circumstances.

~ ~ ~

....and the wife see that she reverence her husband.
Ephesians 5:33

~ ~ ~

Thinking back through the years and the different seasons of our lives, I must admit that, at times, it has not always been easy to sustain my husband. I only mention these times because this is reality. Difficult situations happen to all of us. Many of you can relate, and I know you have walked in my shoes.

The first season of our life together: There were times we were frustrated with each other. We could not communicate spiritually. I had not accepted the Fullness of the Gospel of Jesus Christ in my life, but I did have a strong testimony of Jesus Christ. I did not always understand Gary and how he believed, but I always supported him in his church callings. He never wavered from what he believed, which was a big influence on me. He planted a seed in me to learn more about the Fullness of the Gospel of Jesus Christ.

In another season of our life, we had stepchildren

living with us. I did not always see eye to eye with Gary. Before we married, we had the false assumption that everything would fall into place, and we would be one big happy family. Well, that did not happen.

There was the season when he was a counselor to two bishops, and then he was the bishop. I remember we were asked to come in for an interview with the stake president (a stake president is a leader of a stake, and a stake is a group of congregations). The stake president asked me if I would sustain Gary in the calling as bishop. I said, "Yes, most certainly!" As time went along, reality began to set in. He was taken away from me for long periods so he could meet the demands of being a bishop. I did not always understand when his callings took him away from me.

This happens to all of us. What do we do? We express how we feel, we repent, and we start all over trying to do those things we know we should do.

We are now living in another season of our life. Currently, Gary is living with physical limitations. Do I still sustain my husband? Of course, I do. I find myself helping him.

We have found ourselves growing and becoming stronger people through this time in our lives. He is still my companion, and he is still my friend. We can feel the Spirit in our home.

I respect Gary in many ways, but I have the utmost respect for him in the highest calling of all—his priesthood calling and his ability to lead us spiritually. His desire to study, learn, and grow spiritually has helped him and me to become better people.

In reviewing the meaning of the word sustain, I begin to realize that my responsibility as a wife lies in:
- Being a help to Gary
- Being a source of strength to him
- To comfort him when he is down
- To encourage him
- And to see him through

~ ~ ~

Before we were married, one of the things that attracted me to Gary was his deep faith in his Lord and Savior Jesus Christ. I think of the ways he has sustained me through the years. One of the ways Gary has sustained me: He has had the initiative to lead us spiritually in our home. He has always helped me grow my testimony of my Lord and Savior Jesus Christ. He has encouraged me to read my scriptures, we share spiritual thoughts, and we pray together in our home. I need that! I need someone to guide me and lead me spiritually.

Gary has always sustained me in my callings over the years. He has always shown his love and support for me. When I fail at something, he gently reminds me I can do better.

I find that we sustain each other. I sustain him and he sustains me.

I refer to my husband living with limitations. My husband has three life-altering and life-threatening diseases. He has Myasthenia Gravis, Colon Cancer, and Cushing's Disease.

GARY'S DEFINITION OF MYASTHENIA GRAVIS

Myasthenia Gravis is an autoimmune disease. My brain sends signals to my voluntary muscles, but those signals are blocked by antibodies. The muscles cannot respond to doing something that is blocked. The muscles themselves are not damaged. They are fine. The antibodies are blocking the muscles from working.

COLON CANCER

When Gary had colon cancer surgery, his primary care doctor asked him, "How are you getting through this?" Gary replied without hesitation, "My faith!"

DEFINITION OF CUSHING'S DISEASE

Cushing's Disease is a disease that affects the hormones in your body which can cause uncontrolled weight gain, uncontrolled diabetic numbers, osteoporosis, a large abdomen, and mood changes.

GOD'S GRACE

Although I know my husband is far from perfect, I respect him for trying to live the gospel of Jesus Christ every day in his life. I believe that is what Heavenly Father expects of each of us. We are to put forth an effort to try our best. When we make an error, we get on our knees and repent. We get back up and try all over again! We will never be perfect in this life, but this is where His grace comes in. If we try our best, Heavenly Father makes up the difference for us. The keywords are: After all we can do, Heavenly Father does the rest for us.

In a Sacrament meeting, we renew sacred covenants we have made with Heavenly Father to always remember Him and keep His commandments, and we are willing to take upon us the name of Christ so His Spirit will be with us.

~ ~ ~

This talk was given by my husband, Gary Robinson, in a Sacrament Meeting.

55 T-BIRD TALK

I would like to say something that might inspire a change in each of us.

My passion is cars. I grew up in the 1960's muscle car era. We did not have computers, smartphones, or video games. Your identity was what you drove. I wanted to be cool. I had a bright red 1955 Chevy Bel Air 2-door hardtop with a V-8 engine.

Of course, there was a young man in high school who was cooler. His name was Jerry, and he had a 1955 Thunderbird. This was Ford's answer to the Corvette. It had a V-8, 2-seater, convertible, and hardtop. It was popular and very desirable. They almost killed the Corvette since they sold about 20,401.

I thought Jerry's car was cool. The other guys thought his car was cool, and the girls thought his car was cool.

I never got to drive or even sit in his T-Bird. Jerry

was an upperclassman and ran with a different group. Jerry was very typical of a 1960's young man. He had a lead foot and was a showoff.

Sure enough, it wasn't long before Jerry wrecked his car. Very badly too! His insurance company wanted to total it, pay him off, and scrap it. Jerry, however, knew what he had. His car was ten years old, but a classic already. He wouldn't settle—he wanted his car rebuilt.

He fought the insurance company for a whole year. His sacrifice was: no car for a year, he had to double date, bum rides, and use his mom's rambler. That was a big deal for a teenage boy.

He committed to getting his car rebuilt and eventually, the insurance company settled, and they fixed his car. This car was a treasure to him.

I would like to liken this story to us.

Like Jerry, we have a valuable treasure within our grasp. Like Jerry, we are in the fight of our lives for that treasure. Unlike Jerry's T-Bird, our treasure is not broken or tarnished, and it can be lost. Our treasure is the gift of eternal life with our Father in Heaven and our Savior.

Our adversary is not an insurance company who disagrees with a policyholder. We are up against Satan himself, and he is doing everything he can to prevent us from receiving what the Father has offered us.

In my forty years as a member of this church, I have seen many spiritual miracles among the saints. Some give up before receiving their treasure. This grieves me. Some fall into transgression, some give up because of hard challenges, and some just fade away.

I don't know if Jerry had someone fighting for him (an attorney or his dad), but he probably did. He was only eighteen or nineteen.

We do have an advocate fighting for us. We have Christ who has atoned for us, through repentance He has forgiven us of our sins, cleansed, and strengthened us, making us ready for eternal life in His kingdom. Because of His Atonement, we can win this fight.

Here are some suggestions to help us endure the struggle and to prevail:

- We need to realize what is being offered and desire it. As a young man, worldly things got in my way, and I didn't think about eternal life. Ever so gradually, it has become very important to me.
- Acknowledge you can't obtain eternal life all by yourself. It is only through our Savior Jesus Christ and having faith in Him.
- Read our scriptures. I see miracles when I immerse myself in the scriptures, and I see distance when I slack off. I read my scriptures every morning before I leave for work.
- Repent: Those sins don't go away unless we repent.

- Forgive: Forgiving is hard, and I realize this commandment does apply to me. In our Addiction Recovery Meetings, we make a list of all those we have bad feelings for.
- Attend the temple: I just recently visited with a young man who has had some very hard struggles. He now works in the temple two or three times every month. I could feel his strength and goodness as he spoke to me.
- Do His will: Let go of pride and seek humility. When we insist on doing what we want to do rather than what God wants us to do, we are in opposition to God. If you are in opposition to God, you will lose the fight for eternal life.

If we put our heart into doing those things that God wants us to do, and we don't give up, we will win the fight and gain the prize. Our prize won't be a worldly treasure like Jerry's T-Bird, which could be rusted away by now. Our prize will be eternal life. It is worth fighting for. It is worth making every sacrifice.

If you will hearken to the counsel from the Apostle Paul, *"Fight the good fight of faith, lay hold on eternal life."* 1 Timothy 6:12

Then you can say at the end as the Apostle Paul did, *"I have fought a good fight, I have finished my course, I have kept the faith."* 2 Timothy 4:7

The reason I spoke about fighting to win eternal life is because of the thrill I get when I see individuals come to Christ, live faithful lives, hang on to the end, and never give up the fight. My prayer is that each of you will be able to say, "I have fought a good fight, I have finished my course, I have kept the faith."

I hope you pray that for me too.

You've Been Good for Me

Today is our anniversary! As I look back on my life, I am beginning to realize that I have been given the freedom to grow as a person and the freedom to grow spiritually.

Before I was married, no one could have told me these two things would be the most valuable components of my marriage. I would not have known to look for them in my life.

TOMORROW

Thirty-six years ago today changed our lives.
You asked me to marry you.
I felt joy in my heart on that day,
and we began to plan our future together.

The song, which means I love you and you help me
fly higher than I ever could without you,
was our song, and it is still our song.
We have traveled a long way down the road of life
together
you and me.

We both have had heartaches and disappointments.
We have been there for each other.
Oh! But there has also been much happiness.
Because of my love for you, I will continue to walk
with you.

No matter how hard it is, no matter how long it takes,
no matter what we must face,
I have hope for a tomorrow where life will be much
better than it is here—
a tomorrow where we will be together forever.

I am one of the fortunate ones. With God's direction, I have found what I was looking for. God has given me the person who is best for me. He gave me you!

~ ~ ~

Marry the person who knows you as you are, respects you, and encourages you to pursue your dreams.

~ ~ ~

I am now living in the twilight years of my life. I recently looked into a mirror, and I noticed a few wrinkles around my eyes. Gary said, "Your wrinkles make you very pretty. A mature woman is beautiful."

~ ~ ~

Youth! Where did you go? One moment you are here, and when I turn around, I find you are gone.

A CAREGIVER'S PRAYER

When all hope is gone
and there is no song left to be sung,
I look up to heaven and ask,
"Lord, please renew thy Spirit within me."

During the last few years, I have become a caregiver to my husband. At times, I have felt sorry for myself! I have felt I have missed out on so much in life. Then I reminded myself: Gary did not ask this for himself. This is not his choice. He, too, is having a hard time. He, also, is missing out on so much in life.

These are questions I ask myself:

Is it always easy for me?

Are there times I want to quit?

Do I have to sacrifice my life for him?

Do I, at times, stretch my mind beyond the capacity I currently know?

Do I ever have tears?

Do I ask Heavenly Father to help me?

Am I grateful for others when they show me they care?

Do I have more understanding and compassion for others who are caregivers?

Do I always understand?

Have I become a bitter person, or have I become a better person?

As I stop and ponder my feelings during this difficult time, these words come to my mind—words spoken to my children—words from another time, another place, another season in my life. These words ring out loud and clear to me: The good times far outweigh the bad times, and it is the memories of the good times that keep me moving forward through this rough patch.

A LETTER TO MY HUSBAND

I have carried the weight of an unforgiving heart with me day after day. This weight consists of the bad feelings I have had that have been the result of your illness. I want to hang on to them and not let them go. Those feelings made me validate the lie that I made up in my mind that because of your actions, I was more righteous than you.

Then one day, I read a book about a young woman who had always blamed her father for the death of her mother. It was not until her father died that the woman, now older, realized the truth. Her father was not to blame for her mother's death. He was only trying to protect his daughter from the truth. The truth was that her mother was an alcoholic, and her father was trying to stop her mother from leaving. She left anyway, and she was killed in a car accident.

I don't want to be like this unforgiving woman who spent her whole life unjustly blaming her father. I want to release this unforgiving heart. I want to be free—free from these shackles that hold me back— these shackles hold me back from the joy and happiness that I have been robbed.

Just because I want to hang on to my unforgiving heart and all the feelings I have felt as a caregiver, I have not been the daughter that Heavenly Father wants me to be. He wants me to be free of the weight I have felt. He wants me to let my light shine so that others can see the light of truth. He wants me to share with others those things I have come to know are true, and He, also, wants me to continually seek for truth.

One day, I was ready to ask Heavenly Father for forgiveness for the bad feelings I was carrying and let go of the blame and the lies that I had formed in my mind of what I thought was true. He miraculously lifted those bad feelings from my heart so that I am free—free to be the person He wants me to be—free to shine in a world of darkness. In Him there are no lies and there is no darkness. In Him there is only the light of truth. We find truth only when we seek it. We feel joy and much happiness when we find it.

The truth is that because of your emotional illness, a result of your Cushing's Disease, you are not held accountable for your actions. I can see that you still have a deep faith in Jesus Christ as your Lord and Savior, and your hope for eternal life has not diminished. You wish to do good, but at this time in your life, you are limited.

The load that I have carried around for so long has become much lighter only because I was willing to ask forgiveness from Heavenly Father, and I was ready and willing to let go of this heavy load.

A repentant heart always requires forgiveness to be forgiven.

~ ~ ~

I, the Lord, will forgive whom I will forgive, but of you it is required to forgive all men.
Doctrine and Covenants 64:10

THIS PATH WAS CHOSEN FOR ME

My friend, Marianne, taught the lesson in Relief Society today. She asked four sisters this question, "What does holiness look like in your life?" I was selected to be one of the four participants. We each took our turn in answering this question.

This was my answer:

My husband has been very ill over the past few years, and I have been his caregiver. He has suffered a lot of pain, and he has had an emotional illness which he has not always been easy to live with. My life has been very hard at times, and I search for a meaning of why I am in this circumstance.

When I was young, I always dreamed of growing old with the person that I loved, holding hands, sharing our thoughts and our dreams, reading our scriptures together, and enjoying the last few years of our life with each other. Gary's illness has been a change of events for us, and his illness took that dream away from me.

I search for good, and I try to find answers to why I am in this circumstance. I try to look for ways that I have changed for good. All my life I have never wanted to become an old and bitter woman.

After contemplating these thoughts, I realize some of the ways I have changed:

- I have tried to stay positive and not dwell on the negatives. There definitely have been many negatives.

- I have learned to be truly happy for others, especially when they can do those things that I cannot at this time in my life.
- I have learned a lot about sacrifice because I have had to sacrifice my life for my husband. I have had to give up my time and my personal freedom for him.
- Because my husband has not always been the best patient, I have had to learn to forgive.
- Last of all, I have learned to do hard things which, in turn, has made me a stronger person.

In looking over the past few years, I can see there are times when the bad things that happen to us can turn into good things that happen to us.

FOOTPRINTS IN THE SNOW

Where have you gone? I do not know.
I miss you!
I have so many thoughts and questions
that are twirling in my head.

Your influence over me has been for good.
You have led me by example.
You have had the desire to do good.
God has blessed us even though life has not always
been easy.

Where are you?
Why am I left alone?
How do I follow you?
I want to follow you wherever you go.

Then I realize . . .
I am left alone on this mortal earth just for a season.
But I can feel your presence
when I teach others those things you have taught me.

You have left your footprints on the path before me.
I can follow closely behind you
because your footprints are easy to find.
For this reason, I liken the visibility of your footprints
to footprints in the fresh fallen snow.

~ ~ ~

You have led me to where I am now.

To be loved, admired, respected, and accepted for the person we each are with all our weaknesses and our strengths, is that reaching out beyond our grasp? Is that not reaching into heaven itself?

And, if by chance, we were given this request, would you also believe there is a divine being as the giver of this great gift?

As I move forward on my journey seeking eternal life, I find myself alone. I do not feel alone, for I know you are with me because I can feel your presence. I look around, and I see the world turning dark. Yet, I can see a light shining brightly amidst the darkness. This light is the light of Christ, and I have faith this light will always lead me even when my path becomes too dark for me to see.

ACKNOWLEDGMENTS

Thank you, Brian Zahn. I am grateful for the advice you have given me in the final stages of my book. Thank you for your help. Thank you, Connie Martin, for your love and support through the years and for encouraging me to move forward on my journey to publish my book. Jessica Olson, I appreciate you! Any time I had a question, you were always so sweet and willing to help me.

Thank you, Sharon Kizziah-Holmes, for helping me, once again, to fulfill my lifelong dream of becoming a published author.

ABOUT THE AUTHOR

Janet Robinson resides in Southwest Missouri. She considers her life a journey, and a part of her journey is her passion for writing. *Reaching for the Roses* is Janet's third book. She is also the author of *Undying Embers of God's Love* and *The Birth of a New Dawn in Me*. She is currently working on her fourth book. At the end of each book that Janet writes, she feels a chapter has closed in her life.

Janet's grandchildren are one of her greatest joys in life!

www.ingramcontent.com/pod-product-compliance
Lightning Source LLC
Chambersburg PA
CBHW061332040426
42444CB00011B/2876